TEAM SPIRIT ®

SMART BOOKS FOR YOUNG FANS

THE LOS ANGELES LAKERS

BY
MARK STEWART

NORWOODHOUSE PRESS
CHICAGO, ILLINOIS

Norwood House Press
P.O. Box 316598
Chicago, Illinois 60631

For information regarding Norwood House Press, please visit our website at:
www.norwoodhousepress.com or call 866-565-2900.

All photos courtesy of Associated Press except the following:
Macfadden Publishing (6, 9, 37 left), Black Book Partners (11, 28, 38, 41, 43 right),
Topps, Inc. (15, 21, 34 right, 42 top, 45), Author's Collection (16, 28),
Beckett Publications, Inc. (23), Minneapolis/Los Angeles Lakers (30, 31, 33, 40),
Bowman Gum Co. (34 left), National Basketball Association (37 right), The Star Company (42 bottom).
Cover Photo: Mark J. Terrill/Associated Press

The memorabilia and artifacts pictured in this book are presented for educational and informational purposes,
and come from the collection of the author.

Editor: Mike Kennedy
Designer: Ron Jaffe
Project Management: Black Book Partners, LLC.
Special thanks to Topps, Inc.

Library of Congress Cataloging-in-Publication Data

Stewart, Mark, 1960 July 7-
  The Los Angeles Lakers / by Mark Stewart.
    pages cm. -- (Team spirit)
  Includes bibliographical references and index.
  Summary: "A revised Team Spirit Basketball edition featuring the Los
Angeles Lakers that chronicles the history and accomplishments of the team.
Includes access to the Team Spirit website which provides additional
information and photos"-- Provided by publisher.
  ISBN 978-1-59953-635-4 (library edition : alk. paper) -- ISBN
978-1-60357-644-4 (ebook)
  1. Los Angeles Lakers (Basketball team)--History--Juvenile literature. I.
Title.
  GV885.52.L67S74 2014
  796.323'640979494--dc23

                                    2014006549

253N—072014
Manufactured in the United States of America in North Mankato, Minnesota.

COVER PHOTO: The Lakers are one of the most exciting teams in basketball history.
Their players know how important team spirit is to their success.

Table of Contents

ABOUT OUR GLOSSARY

In this book, there may be several words that you are reading for the first time. Some are sports words, some are new vocabulary words, and some are familiar words that are used in an unusual way. All of these words are defined on page 46. Throughout the book, sports words appear in **bold type**. Regular vocabulary words appear in ***bold italic type***.

Meet the Lakers

Most basketball fans expect their favorite team to go through ups and downs. Some years are good, and some years aren't. That simply won't do for fans of the Los Angeles Lakers. They have come to expect teams loaded with talent, and coaches who know how to win.

This *tradition* began in the 1940s, when the Lakers played in an entirely different part of the United States. In the 1960s, they moved west to California. Ever since that day, the **National Basketball Association (NBA)** has truly been "national."

This book tells the story of the Lakers. They are known as a glamorous team, but don't let that fool you. Los Angeles wins with talent, teamwork, focus, and energy. Of course, the Lakers can't help but crack a few smiles along the way. That's why it's so much fun to root for them.

Kobe Bryant flips a pass to Pau Gasol. The Lakers are at their best when they combine talent, teamwork, and energy.

Glory Days

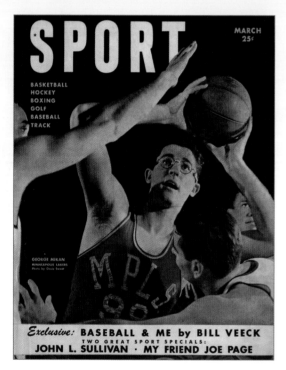

BASKETBALL HOCKEY BOXING GOLF BASEBALL TRACK

SPORT

MARCH 25¢

GEORGE MIKAN
MINNEAPOLIS LAKERS
Photo by Ozzie Sweet

Exclusive: **BASEBALL & ME by BILL VEECK**
TWO GREAT SPORT SPECIALS:
JOHN L. SULLIVAN · MY FRIEND JOE PAGE

Did you ever stop and wonder how the Lakers got their name? The team's story actually began in Minneapolis, Minnesota. The state is known as the "land of 10,000 lakes," and the cargo ships that work Lake Superior are sometimes called "lakers."

The Lakers joined the **National Basketball League (NBL)** in 1947. They were led by coach John Kundla and forward Jim Pollard. Two weeks into their first season, the Lakers added George Mikan, a hulking center known to every basketball fan in America. Mikan wore thick glasses that made him look like Clark Kent. But he played like Superman. Mikan and Pollard led the Lakers to the NBL championship that spring.

For the 1948–49 season, the Lakers moved to the **Basketball Association of America (BAA)**. The BAA played in large cities and was a rival of the NBL, which had teams in smaller towns. The Lakers promptly won the BAA championship. The following season, the NBL and BAA joined forces to become the NBA. Once again, the Lakers won the championship.

The Lakers put together an unbeatable lineup. Kundla stressed unselfish play, and Minneapolis became known for its teamwork on offense and defense. Mikan and Pollard shared the front line with Vern Mikkelsen. Slater Martin ran the offense from the backcourt. From 1947–48 to 1953–54, the Lakers won a championship in every season but one.

Amazingly, it would take almost 20 years for the Lakers to win another championship. By then, the team had moved west to Los Angeles. The Lakers'

long "drought" was not for lack of talent. During the 1960s, they had two game-changing superstars—Elgin Baylor and

LEFT: George Mikan towers over defenders on the cover of this 1948 *Sport Magazine*.   **ABOVE**: Jim Pollard scores an easy basket against the New York Knicks.

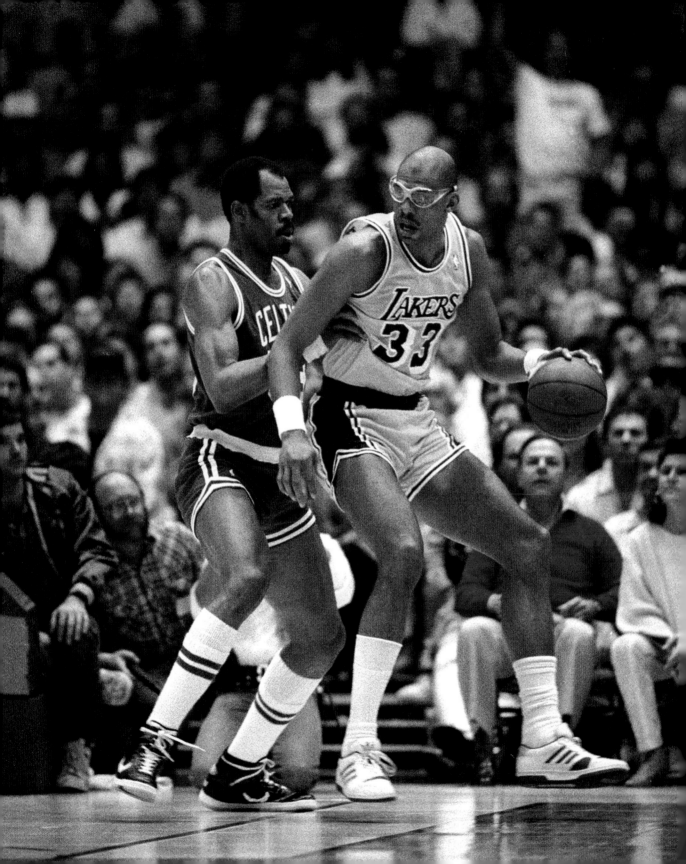

Jerry West. Baylor used his quickness and leaping ability to put up dazzling scoring numbers. West had a deadly long-range shot and the size and speed to drive straight through opposing defenses. The Lakers reached the **NBA Finals** seven times in nine seasons, but they fell short of a championship each time.

Finally, in 1972, Los Angeles captured its first NBA crown. West and center Wilt Chamberlain led a team that won an amazing 69 games during the regular season. The Lakers then beat the New York Knicks for their first championship since their days in Minneapolis.

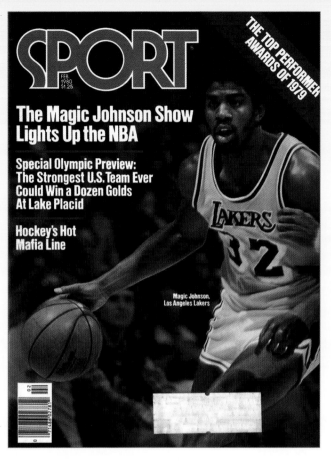

The Lakers returned to the top of the NBA in the 1980s, with a team that featured Magic Johnson, James Worthy, and Kareem Abdul-Jabbar. Johnson was a 6' 9" guard with great passing skills. Worthy was a strong, agile forward. Abdul-Jabbar was one of the greatest centers in history. From 1979–80 to 1990–91,

LEFT: Kareem Abdul-Jabbar works his way into scoring position.
ABOVE: Magic Johnson lit up the league in the 1980s.

Los Angeles reached the NBA Finals nine times and won five championships. This team liked to speed up the game and overwhelm opponents. Coach Pat Riley called this style "Showtime."

In the late-1990s, the Lakers rebuilt around two players who reminded longtime fans of Chamberlain and West. Los Angeles traded for center Shaquille O'Neal and **drafted** guard Kobe Bryant straight out of high school. Bryant's father, Joe, had been a star in the NBA and also in Europe. Like Magic, Kobe combined the size of a forward and the skills of a guard.

Under coach Phil Jackson, O'Neal and Bryant led the Lakers to the NBA championship three times, in 2000, 2001, and 2002. In 2004, Jackson stepped down as coach and O'Neal was traded away. When the Lakers struggled, Jackson returned to the sidelines and rebuilt the team around Bryant and a group of talented **veterans** that included Lamar Odom, Derek Fisher, Pau Gasol, and Ron Artest. The Lakers won two more league titles, in 2009 and 2010.

In the years that followed, Los Angeles struggled to match that success. Jackson left the team for good, and Bryant began to show his age. The Lakers started to look to the future. Their fans can't wait until another collection of stars brings the NBA crown back to L.A.

LEFT: Shaquille O'Neal scores on a dunk. **ABOVE**: Kobe Bryant led the Lakers to the NBA championship five times.

Home Court

Before their move west, the Lakers played in the Minneapolis Auditorium, in the city's downtown area. After arriving in California, the team used the Los Angeles Memorial Sports Arena and the Great Western Forum. Ringed by Roman columns, the Forum was one of the fanciest sports arenas in the country.

In 1999, the Lakers moved into a new arena in downtown Los Angeles. Every seat has a great view of the court. Outside of the building are larger-than-life statues of Magic Johnson, Jerry West, Kareem Abdul-Jabbar, announcer Chick Hearn, hockey star Wayne Gretzky, and boxer Oscar de la Hoya.

BY THE NUMBERS

- *The Lakers' arena has 18,997 seats for basketball.*

- *An eight-sided scoreboard hangs above the court.*

- *As of 2013–14, the Lakers had retired nine numbers— 13 (Wilt Chamberlain), 22 (Elgin Baylor), 25 (Gail Goodrich), 32 (Magic Johnson), 33 (Kareem Abdul-Jabbar), 34 (Shaquille O'Neal), 42 (James Worthy), 44 (Jerry West), and 52 (Jamaal Wilkes).*

Confetti flutters down on the Lakers' home court after the team's 2000 championship.

Dressed for Success

For much of their early history, the Lakers' colors were bright blue and white, which reminded fans of the water and sky. The team name was spelled out in block letters on the light-colored tops of the home uniform. On the road, *MPLS* (short for Minneapolis) was sometimes used across the front of the jerseys.

The Lakers kept their blue and white colors for many years after moving to Los Angeles. In the late-1960s, the team switched to purple and gold. In recent years, the Lakers have worn white home uniforms on occasion. They also dress in a black uniform for special games. The team *logo* has remained almost the same since 1960.

VERN **MIKKELSEN** MINN. Lakers

LEFT: Pau Gasol wears the team's white uniform in a 2013–14 game.
ABOVE: This trading card of Vern Mikkelsen shows the Lakers' bright blue uniform.

We Won!

Between 1948 and 1950, when the Lakers played in Minneapolis, they made basketball fans rethink what it meant to be a championship team. Early in 1948, the Lakers won the World **Professional** Basketball Tournament. This competition attracted the best teams from around the country, including the top African American clubs. In the final, George Mikan scored 40 points against the New York Rens in a 75–71 victory.

A few months later, the Lakers advanced to the finals of the National Basketball League. They beat the Rochester Royals in four games. The following season, the Lakers joined the Basketball Association of America. They reached the finals and beat the Washington Capitols in six games.

In 1949–50, the NBL and BAA joined forces to become the NBA. The Lakers won 51 games and defeated the Syracuse Nationals to become the new league's first champion. That gave Minneapolis three titles in three different leagues in three years!

The Lakers had it all. Mikan was an unstoppable center. Jim Pollard and Vern Mikkelsen were excellent scorers and rebounders. Guard Slater Martin was a fantastic playmaker and an aggressive defender. This group continued to win championships, including three more in a row beginning in 1951–52.

The Lakers' next championship came in 1971–72, 11 years after the team moved to Los Angeles. The Lakers featured a mix of old and young stars, including Jerry West, Wilt Chamberlain, Gail Goodrich, Jim McMillian, and Happy Hairston. They also had experienced bench players in Pat Riley, Flynn Robinson, and Leroy Ellis. The Lakers won 69 games that season—including

LEFT: Slater Martin signed this photo from the early 1950s.
ABOVE: Wilt Chamberlain tries one of his famous "finger roll" shots against the Knicks in the 1972 NBA Finals.

33 in a row—and beat the New York Knicks in the NBA Finals. West, who had been with the team since 1960, finally won his first championship.

The Lakers began building a new *dynasty* in the late 1970s. They traded for Kareem Abdul-Jabbar and Jamaal Wilkes, and drafted Magic Johnson and James Worthy. These four stars helped Los Angeles become the best team of the 1980s. The Lakers met the Philadelphia 76ers in the NBA Finals in 1980 and 1982. They won both times. Los Angeles won two more titles against the Boston Celtics, in 1985 and 1987. The teams were bitter *rivals*, so these championships were extremely satisfying.

Los Angeles faced a new opponent in the 1988 NBA Finals. The Detroit Pistons were a tough, physical team, but they couldn't keep up with coach Pat Riley's Showtime offense. Riley was in charge for four of the five championships during this stretch.

The Lakers returned to the NBA Finals twice more. Johnson and Worthy were still the leaders in Los Angeles. They were joined by Byron Scott, Sam Perkins, Vlade Divac, and A.C. Green. But as the 1990s drew to a close, the Lakers were no longer a serious championship **contender**.

By 1999–2000, the Lakers had retooled. Phil Jackson was now the coach, and Kobe Bryant and Shaquille O'Neal were his two top stars. Jackson surrounded them with excellent role players,

Kobe Bryant and Shaquille O'Neal celebrate their 2000 NBA championship.

including Rick Fox, Derek Fisher, and Robert Horry. Los Angeles defeated the Indiana Pacers in the 2000 NBA Finals. The following year, the Lakers beat the 76ers in five games for the championship. In 2002, they swept the New Jersey Nets for their third title in four years.

Many fans wondered whether Bryant was a strong enough leader to win an NBA title without O'Neal. They found out after Los Angeles traded the big center to the Miami Heat. In 2007–08, Bryant was named the NBA's **Most Valuable Player (MVP)**. A year later, he led a talented supporting cast that included Pau Gasol, Andrew Bynum, and Lamar Odom into the NBA Finals. Los Angeles won in five games, and Bryant was named the series MVP.

The Lakers earned their 15th NBA championship in 2009–10. It came against the Celtics in a showdown that reminded fans of the great battles between the teams in the 1980s. Bryant had another great series and was voted the MVP once again.

Go-To Guys

To be a true star in the NBA, you need more than a great shot. You have to be a "go-to guy"—someone teammates trust to make the winning play when the seconds are ticking away in a big game. Lakers fans have had a lot to cheer about over the years, including these great stars …

THE PIONEERS

GEORGE MIKAN   6′ 10″ Center

- BORN: 6/18/1924   • DIED: 6/1/2005
- PLAYED FOR TEAM: 1947–48 TO 1953–54 & 1955–56

George Mikan used his massive body to back opponents toward the rim, where he could shoot a hook or layup with either hand. Mikan was so hard to defend that the NBA changed its own rules. The league widened the foul lane and created the **3-second rule**, which made it more difficult for all big men to score.

JIM POLLARD   6′ 4″ Forward

- BORN: 7/9/1922   • DIED: 1/22/1993   • PLAYED FOR TEAM: 1947–48 TO 1954–55

Jim Pollard was nicknamed "The Kangaroo Kid." He was a great leaper and an excellent scorer. When opponents tried to crowd around George Mikan, Pollard was often left wide open for easy shots and rebounds.

SLATER MARTIN 5′ 10″ Guard

• BORN: 10/22/1925 • DIED: 10/18/2012 • PLAYED FOR TEAM: 1949–50 TO 1955–56

In the early days of pro basketball, point guards handled the ball much more than they do today. That made Slater Martin the key to the Lakers' early success. He was a quick and clever guard who triggered the offense.

ELGIN BAYLOR 6′ 5″ Forward

• BORN: 9/16/1934 • PLAYED FOR TEAM: 1958–59 TO 1971–72

Elgin Baylor brought a whole new brand of basketball to the NBA. He soared over opponents for dunks and rebounds. Baylor's high-flying, twisting shots captured the imagination of young players and fans.

JERRY WEST 6′ 3″ Guard

• BORN: 5/28/1938

• PLAYED FOR TEAM: 1960–61 TO 1973–74

Jerry West was one of history's greatest all-around players. He was famous for making shots in close games. West's nickname was "Mr. Clutch."

WILT CHAMBERLAIN 7′ 1″ Center

• BORN: 8/21/1936 • DIED: 10/12/1999 • PLAYED FOR TEAM: 1968–69 TO 1972–73

Wilt Chamberlain might have been the greatest athlete in NBA history. Opponents were helpless against him. The Lakers went to the NBA Finals four times in his five years in Los Angeles.

ABOVE: Jerry West

KAREEM ABDUL-JABBAR · 7′ 2″ Center

- BORN: 4/16/1947 · PLAYED FOR TEAM: 1975–76 TO 1988–89

Kareem Abdul-Jabbar was the NBA's best center when the Lakers traded for him. He helped them win five championships and was named MVP three times along the way. Abdul-Jabbar retired as the NBA's all-time leading scorer with 38,387 points.

MAGIC JOHNSON · 6′ 9″ Guard

- BORN: 8/14/1959 · PLAYED FOR TEAM: 1979–80 TO 1990–91 & 1995–96

Magic Johnson was unlike any player before him—a point guard in a big man's body. His ability to get all his teammates involved in a game made him one of the best leaders in NBA history. Johnson led the NBA in **assists** four times and in steals twice.

JAMES WORTHY · 6′ 9″ Forward

- BORN: 2/27/1961
- PLAYED FOR TEAM: 1982–83 TO 1993–94

James Worthy was one of the best all-around forwards ever to play in the NBA. When the Lakers ran their fast break, Worthy often finished it off with a dunk. He was the MVP of the 1988 NBA Finals.

SHAQUILLE O'NEAL 7′ 1″ Center

- BORN: 3/6/1972
- PLAYED FOR TEAM: 1996–97 TO 2003–04

Shaquille O'Neal was a man in search of a championship when he joined the Lakers. He was the league's most unstoppable player, but he needed a great team to support him. "Shaq" found that and more in Los Angeles, where he won three NBA titles.

KOBE BRYANT 6′ 7″ Guard

- BORN: 8/23/1978
- FIRST SEASON WITH TEAM: 1996–97

Kobe Bryant joined the Lakers as a teenager. Within a few seasons, he was one of the top players in the NBA. Bryant was voted the MVP of the **All-Star Game** three times.

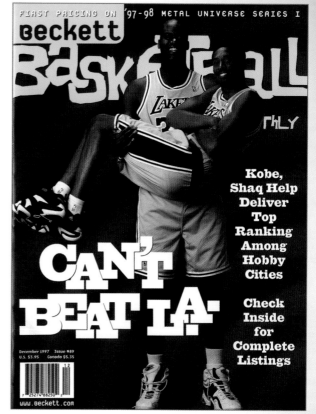

PAU GASOL 7′ 0″ Center

- BORN: 7/6/1980   • FIRST SEASON WITH TEAM: 2007–08

After Shaquille O'Neal left the Lakers, they traded for Pau Gasol. He blended perfectly with his Los Angeles teammates, especially Kobe Bryant. Gasol helped the Lakers win two NBA titles and was an **All-Star** three years in a row for Los Angeles.

LEFT: James Worthy **ABOVE**: This magazine cover said it all about the Lakers with Shaquille O'Neal and Kobe Bryant.

Calling the Shots

A winning basketball team needs more than great players. It also requires a coach who knows how to get the best out of those players. The Lakers have one of the most impressive coaching traditions in basketball history. Their first coach was John Kundla. He believed that a pro team needed a high-scoring center to win. Kundla guided the Lakers to six championships.

During the 1960s, Fred Schaus coached the Lakers. His lineup featured Elgin Baylor and Jerry West, but the team could not find a dependable center. Even so, Schaus led the club to the NBA Finals four times in a five-year period. Bill Sharman—a star for the great Boston Celtics teams—was hired in 1971 to shake things up. He guided the Lakers to the NBA title in his first year calling the shots.

From 1979–80 to 1990–91, the Lakers made it to the NBA Finals nine times under three coaches—Paul Westhead, Mike Dunleavy, and Pat Riley. No one was more committed to winning than Riley. His Showtime style made great use of Magic Johnson's unique talents. The Lakers won the NBA championship four times under Riley.

In 1999, Los Angeles hired Phil Jackson to coach the team. Jackson had already won six championships with the Chicago Bulls. With the Lakers, his main challenge was getting his two superstars, Shaquille O'Neal and Kobe Bryant, to work together for the good of the team. Jackson led the Lakers to the NBA title in each of his first three seasons. After O'Neal was traded to the Miami Heat, Jackson rebuilt the club around Bryant. The Lakers went on to win two more championships before Jackson retired in 2011.

LEFT: John Kundla rides off the court on George Mikan's shoulders.
ABOVE: Phil Jackson offers advice to Kobe Bryant.

One Great Day

Few scorers in NBA history could match Kobe Bryant's artistry or explosiveness. When he was in the zone, it seemed there was no stopping him. That was the case on a January night in 2006 in Los Angeles against the Toronto Raptors.

Bryant was making shots from everywhere on the court—long **3-pointers**, pull-up jump shots, driving layups, and monster dunks. At halftime, he had 26 points. The Lakers, by contrast, were struggling. Toronto held a 63–49 lead.

In the third quarter Los Angeles kept giving the ball to Bryant, and he kept scoring. Slowly but surely, the Lakers fought back. They took control of the game in the fourth quarter. Actually, it was Bryant who took control. He scored 55 points in the second half to lead the Lakers to a 122–104 victory. Bryant finished with 81 points!

His feat was truly amazing. The only time an NBA player scored more than 81 points was 44 years earlier, when Wilt Chamberlain

Kobe Bryant floats to the hoop for a basket against the Raptors.

set a record with 100 points. Chamberlain was a center who towered over his opponents, and his team was far ahead in the game. Bryant, on the other hand, was challenged on every shot. "These points tonight mattered," he said after the game. "We needed them."

Did Bryant think he would ever score more points in a game than Michael Jordan, Jerry West, and other great guards? "Not even in my dreams," he smiled.

Legend Has It

Did the Lakers ever swap one Hall of Famer for another?

LEGEND HAS IT that they did. Although the story is a little more complicated. In 1976, future **Hall of Famer** Gail

Goodrich left the Lakers as a **free agent** and joined the New Orleans (now Utah) Jazz. The NBA rules at the time said the Jazz had to give Los Angeles something in return. The Lakers received their first pick in the 1979 draft. When New Orleans finished with the worst record in the league, Los Angeles wound up with the top selection overall. The Lakers used it on Magic Johnson, who joined Goodrich in the Hall of Fame in 2002.

ABOVE: Gail Goodrich makes a move to the basket.

Did the Lakers once play a game with 12-foot rims?

LEGEND HAS IT that they did. The official height of NBA rims is 10 feet. But in a 1954 game between the Lakers and St. Louis Hawks, both teams agreed to play with 12-foot rims. The NBA was experimenting with different ways to speed up games. The Lakers won, but they weren't fans of the higher rims. Altogether, they made only 22 of 77 shots. Slater Martin, the shortest man on the court, had a better idea—lower the rims to six feet. "It would make a George Mikan out of me!" he said.

Which Laker could speak Klingon?

LEGEND HAS IT that James Worthy could. In the break between the 1992–93 and 1993–94 seasons, the 6'9" forward appeared on the television series *Star Trek: The Next Generation*. He played a Klingon named Koral, and needed three hours of makeup before the cameras started rolling. The show's producer says that Worthy was the "tallest Klingon on record."

It Really Happened

Two of the greatest centers in basketball history have played for the Lakers: Wilt Chamberlain and Kareem Abdul-Jabbar. But many fans forget the big man who bridged the gap between the two. His name was Elmore Smith, and he was also known for his great nickname: The Rejector. Smith stood seven feet tall. He used his long arms and jumping ability to block shots in bunches.

The Lakers traded for Smith before the 1973–74 season. In his ninth game, Los Angeles hosted the Portland Trailblazers. It was a wild contest. Six Portland players scored in double-figures. Meanwhile, Gail Goodrich and Jerry West combined for 73 points. The star of the game, however, was Smith. Every time the Trailblazers attacked the basket, Smith was there to challenge them. He swatted away shot after shot.

"It didn't seem like they were catching on," Smith remembers. "They continued to try to score close to the basket and I just kept blocking their shots."

The Lakers pulled away in the fourth quarter to win, 111–98. Smith finished with 17 blocked shots. He also had 12 points and 16 rebounds, giving him a rare **triple-double**. But it was his defensive effort that made headlines. In the years that followed, no one matched his record of 17 blocks.

"There have been a lot of talented guys that I thought would have broken it by now," he says, "but it just didn't happen."

LEFT: Elmore Smith played two seasons in L.A. and led the Lakers in blocks both times.   **ABOVE**: Smith stuffs an opponent's layup attempt.

For the Lakers, playing in front of movie, music, and television celebrities is all part of a night's work. Their home court is only a few miles away from where many of the world's most famous people live and work. The team's most loyal fan is Jack Nicholson, the award-winning actor. He sits in a courtside seat and knows most of the players personally.

Other celebrities who can be seen in the stands include Will Smith, Brad Pitt, Matthew McConaughey, Dustin Hoffman, Snoop Dogg, Alicia Keys, and Sarah Michelle Gellar. These stars love the Lakers, but there is something else they enjoy about going to games. For a few hours, they can relax, be themselves, and cheer for their favorite team just like any other fan.

LEFT: Jack Nicholson and Alicia Keys keep their eyes on the ball at a Lakers game.   **ABOVE**: As this 1950s game program shows, the team was also great fun to watch when it played in Minneapolis.

The basketball season is played from October through June. That means each season takes place at the end of one year and the beginning of the next. In this timeline, the accomplishments of the Lakers are shown by season.

1949–50
The team wins its first NBA championship.

1960–61
The Lakers move to Los Angeles.

1947–48
The Lakers join the NBL.

1958–59
Elgin Baylor is named **Rookie of the Year**.

1971–72
The Lakers win their first title in Los Angeles.

George Mikan led the Lakers in the 1940s and 1950s.

Rudy LaRusso starred for the team after the move west.

Magic Johnson and Pat Riley celebrate one of the team's five titles during the 1980s.

1987–88
The Lakers win their fifth championship of the 1980s.

2001–02
The Lakers sweep the New Jersey Nets in the NBA Finals.

2012–13
Kobe Bryant takes first place on the team's all-time scoring list.

1976–77
Kareem Abdul-Jabbar is named MVP for the second year in a row.

2009–10
The Lakers win their second championship in a row.

2010–11
Lamar Odom is named **Sixth Man of the Year**.

Lamar Odom glides to the basket.

MAN OF ACTION!

Kareem Abdul-Jabbar has appeared on television and in the movies more than 100 times in his life—sometimes as himself and sometimes playing a character. In 2010, he produced the award-winning film *On the Shoulders of Giants*.

THE GRADUATE

In the opening game of the 2005–06 season, Andrew Bynum became the youngest player in NBA history. He took the court for the Lakers four months after his high school graduation—and just six days past his 18th birthday! Bynum had two rebounds and two blocked shots in just over five minutes of play.

CENTER OF ATTENTION

In Game 6 of the 1980 NBA Finals, rookie guard Magic Johnson took the place of injured center Kareem Abdul-Jabbar. He scored 42 points and grabbed 15 rebounds to lead the Lakers to the championship.

TRUE WEST

The red-white-and-blue NBA logo has the outline of a player dribbling a basketball. Many believe that Jerry West was the "model" for this player.

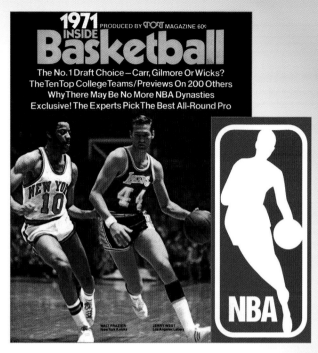

YOU AGAIN?

In 2008 and 2012, Pau Gasol led Spain to the men's basketball finals at the *Olympics*. Both times, his country lost to Team USA, which starred his Lakers teammate, Kobe Bryant.

CALLING LONG DISTANCE

In 2008–09, Vladimir Radmanovic made 60 of his 136 3-point shots for the Lakers. His 44.1 percent shooting from 3-point range set a team record.

WORST TO FIRST

In 1957–58, the Lakers finished dead last in their **division**. That spring, the team picked Elgin Baylor in the draft. In 1958–59, Baylor led the Lakers to the division championship.

ABOVE: Does this magazine cover of Jerry West look like the NBA logo?

Talking Basketball

"Ask not what your teammates can do for you. Ask what you can do for your teammates."

▶ **Magic Johnson,** *on being a good team player*

"The first five times we threw the ball to Mikan, all five guys from the other team went to him!"

▶ **John Kundla,** *on the respect opponents had for George Mikan*

"He was one of the most spectacular shooters the game has ever known."

▶ **Jerry West,** *on Elgin Baylor*

"This is a guy who could and should have been the MVP player for ten consecutive seasons."

▶ **Phil Jackson,** *on Shaquille O'Neal*

"Derek Fisher is my all-time favorite teammate."

▶ **Kobe Bryant,** *on his longtime backcourt mate*

"I started wearing glasses when I was 12, and people told me then that anyone who wore glasses could never be a great athlete … I guess you could say I've always had a burning desire to be successful."

▶ **George Mikan,** *on overcoming obstacles to become a star*

"He only knows one way to play. That's to ***dominate.***"

▶ **James Worthy,** *on Kobe Bryant*

LEFT: Magic Johnson
ABOVE: Phil Jackson diagrams a play for Shaquille O'Neal.

Great Debates

People who root for the Lakers love to compare their favorite moments, teams, and players. Some debates have been going on for years! How would you settle these classic basketball arguments?

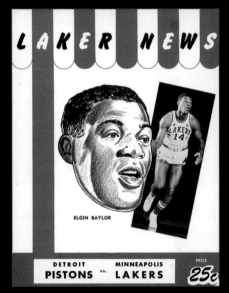

Elgin Baylor was the team's greatest forward ...

... because he was the first to play "above the basket." Baylor's quick moves and incredible leaping ability left defenders in awe as he floated toward the rim. Though he stood just 6' 5", Baylor ( ) set numerous scoring records, including 61 points in Game 5 of the 1962 NBA Finals. Baylor was also a great rebounder, often grabbing 20 or more a game.

Baylor was amazing, but James Worthy was better ...

... because he helped the Lakers do something Baylor never could: win a championship. Worthy could have been a scoring and rebounding leader for any team in the NBA. Instead, he fit his talents into the Lakers' system. Worthy helped Los Angeles win three titles and was named MVP of the 1988 NBA Finals.

The 1972 Lakers would beat the 1987 "Showtime" Lakers in a seven-game series …

… because they were such a *versatile* team. Guards Jerry West and Gail Goodrich were tremendous scorers, forwards Jim McMillian and Happy Hairston were tough all-around players, and Wilt Chamberlain was a monster at center. The 1972 Lakers would have been happy to run with the Showtime offense. They averaged 121 points a game.

Are you kidding? By the second quarter, the 1972 Lakers' tongues would be hanging out …

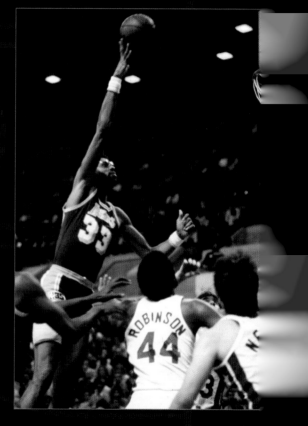

… because the 1987 Lakers were younger, faster, and stronger. The Showtime team had great defenders who made opponents work hard for every shot and rebound, including Kareem Abdul-Jabbar (RIGHT). He would have worn out Chamberlain. The Lakers would not have allowed West and Goodrich to catch their breath, either. It would be close for about 15 minutes, and then

The great Lakers teams and players have left their marks on the record books. These are the "best of the best" …

WILT CHAMBERLAIN
center

LOS ANGELES

Wilt Chamberlain

STAR 85

PAT RILEY
HEAD COACH
Los Angeles Lakers

Pat Riley

LAKERS AWARD WINNERS

NBA FINALS MVP

Jerry West	1968–69
Wilt Chamberlain	1971–72
Magic Johnson	1979–80
Magic Johnson	1981–82
Kareem Abdul-Jabbar	1984–85
Magic Johnson	1986–87
James Worthy	1987–88
Shaquille O'Neal	1999–00
Shaquille O'Neal	2000–01
Shaquille O'Neal	2001–02
Kobe Bryant	2008–09
Kobe Bryant	2009–10

ROOKIE OF THE YEAR

Elgin Baylor	1958–59

SIXTH MAN AWARD

Lamar Odom	2010–11

COACH OF THE YEAR

Bill Sharman	1971–72
Pat Riley	1989–90
Del Harris	1994–95

MOST VALUABLE PLAYER

George Mikan	1947–48*
Kareem Abdul-Jabbar	1975–76
Kareem Abdul-Jabbar	1976–77
Kareem Abdul-Jabbar	1979–80
Magic Johnson	1986–87
Magic Johnson	1988–89
Magic Johnson	1989–90
Shaquille O'Neal	1999–00

ALL-STAR GAME MVP

George Mikan	1952–53
Elgin Baylor	1958–59
Jerry West	1971–72
Magic Johnson	1989–90
Magic Johnson	1991–92
Shaquille O'Neal	1999–00**
Kobe Bryant	2001–02
Shaquille O'Neal	2003–04
Kobe Bryant	2008–09
Kobe Bryant	2010–11

DEFENSIVE PLAYER OF THE YEAR

Michael Cooper	1986–87

* *The Lakers played in the National Basketball League.*
** *Shared award with another player.*

LAKERS ACHIEVEMENTS

ACHIEVEMENT	SEASON
NBL Champions	1947–48
BAA Champions	1948–49
NBA Champions	1949–50
NBA Champions	1951–52
NBA Champions	1952–53
NBA Champions	1953–54
NBA Champions	1971–72
NBA Champions	1979–80
NBA Champions	1981–82
NBA Champions	1984–85
NBA Champions	1986–87
NBA Champions	1987–88
NBA Champions	1999–00
NBA Champions	2000–01
NBA Champions	2001–02
NBA Champions	2008–09
NBA Champions	2009–10

ABOVE: Jim McMillian was a key member of the 1972 champs.
LEFT: George Mikan stands by all the trophies and awards he won with the Lakers in the 1940s and 1950s.

he history of a basketball team is made up of many smaller stories. These stories take place all over the map—not just in the city a team calls "home." Match the pushpins on these maps to the **TEAM FACTS**, and you will begin to see the story of the Lakers unfold!

TEAM FACTS

1. Los Angeles, California—*The Lakers have played here since 1960.*
2. Berkeley, California—*Jamaal Wilkes was born here.*
3. Deer Lodge, Montana—*Phil Jackson was born here.*
4. Minneapolis, Minnesota—*The Lakers played here from 1947 to 1960.*
5. Joliet, Illinois—*George Mikan was born here.*
6. Rome, New York—*Pat Riley was born here.*
7. New York, New York—*Kareem Abdul-Jabbar was born here.*
8. Philadelphia, Pennsylvania—*Kobe Bryant was born here.*
9. Washington, D.C.—*Elgin Baylor was born here.*
10. Gastonia, North Carolina—*James Worthy was born here.*
11. Barcelona, Spain—*Pau Gasol was born here.*
12. Prijepolje, Yugoslavia—*Vlade Divac was born here.*

Vlade Divac

Glossary

Basketball Words
Vocabulary Words

3-POINTERS—Baskets made from behind the 3-point line.

3-SECOND RULE—The rule that prohibits an offensive player from staying more than three seconds in the lane.

ALL-STAR—A player selected to play in the annual All-Star Game.

ALL-STAR GAME—The annual game in which the best players from the East and the West play against each other.

ASSISTS—Passes that lead to baskets.

BASKETBALL ASSOCIATION OF AMERICA (BAA)—The league that started in 1946–47 and later became the NBA.

CONTENDER—A team that competes for a championship.

DIVISION—A group of teams within a league that play in the same part of the country.

DOMINATE—Control completely.

DRAFTED—Chosen from a group of the best college and foreign players. The NBA draft is held each summer.

DYNASTY—A family, group, or team that maintains power over time.

FREE AGENT—A player who is allowed to sign with any team that wants him.

HALL OF FAMER—A player voted into the Hall of Fame, the museum in Springfield, Massachusetts where the game's greatest players are honored.

LOGO—A symbol or design that represents a company or team.

MOST VALUABLE PLAYER (MVP)—The annual award given to the league's best player; also given to the best player in the league finals and All-Star Game.

NATIONAL BASKETBALL ASSOCIATION (NBA)—The professional league that has been operating since 1946–47.

NATIONAL BASKETBALL LEAGUE (NBL)—An early professional league that played 12 seasons, from 1937–38 to 1948–49.

NBA FINALS—The playoff series that decides the champion of the league.

OLYMPICS—An international sports competition held every four years.

PROFESSIONAL—A player or team that plays a sport for money.

RIVALS—Extremely emotional competitors.

ROOKIE OF THE YEAR—The annual award given to the league's best first-year player.

SIXTH MAN OF THE YEAR—The annual award given to the league's best player off the bench.

TRADITION—A belief or custom that is handed down from generation to generation.

TRIPLE-DOUBLE—A game in which a player records double-figures in three different statistical categories.

VERSATILE—Able to do many things well.

VETERANS—Players with great experience.

FAST BREAK

TEAM SPIRIT introduces a great way to stay up to date with your team! Visit our **FAST BREAK** link and get connected to the latest and greatest updates. **FAST BREAK** serves as a young reader's ticket to an exclusive web page—with more stories, fun facts, team records, and photos of the Lakers. Content is updated during and after each season. The **FAST BREAK** feature also enables readers to send comments and letters to the author! Log onto:

www.norwoodhousepress.com/library.aspx

and click on the tab: **TEAM SPIRIT** to access **FAST BREAK**.

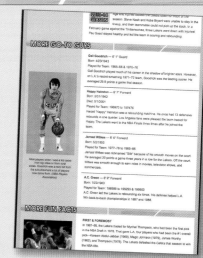

Read all the books in the series to learn more about professional sports. For a complete listing of the baseball, basketball, football, and hockey teams in the **TEAM SPIRIT** series, visit our website at:

www.norwoodhousepress.com/library.aspx

On the Road

LOS ANGELES LAKERS
1111 South Figueroa Street
Los Angeles, California   90015
(310) 426-6000
www.Lakers.com

**NAISMITH MEMORIAL
BASKETBALL HALL OF FAME**
1000 West Columbus Avenue
Springfield, Massachusetts 01105
(877) 4HOOPLA
www.hoophall.com

On the Bookshelf

To learn more about the sport of basketball, look for these books at your library or bookstore:

• Doeden, Matt. *Basketball Legends In the Making*. North Mankato, Minnesota: Capstone Press, 2014.

• Rappaport, Ken. *Basketball's Top 10 Slam Dunkers*. Berkeley Heights, New Jersey: Enslow Publishers, 2013.

• Silverman, Drew. *The NBA Finals*. Minneapolis, Minnesota: ABDO Group, 2013.

Index

PAGE NUMBERS IN **BOLD** REFER TO ILLUSTRATIONS.

THE TEAM

MARK STEWART has written more than 40 books on basketball, and over 150 sports books for kids. He grew up in New York City during the 1960s rooting for the Knicks and Nets, and was lucky enough to meet many of the stars of those teams. Mark comes from a family of writers. His grandfather was Sunday Editor of *The New York Times* and his mother was Articles Editor of *The Ladies' Home Journal* and *McCall's*. Mark has profiled hundreds of athletes over the last 20 years. He has also written several books about his native New York, and New Jersey, his home today. Mark is a graduate of Duke University, with a degree in History. He lives with his daughters and wife Sarah overlooking Sandy Hook, New Jersey.